how to make
(all-in-one, one-size-fits-most)
cloth diapers

jennifer c. berry

CONTENTS

INTRODUCTION

When I first started looking into cloth diapering, I was overwhelmed by all the options. And – let's be honest – the price. Twenty dollars for one diaper?! Okay, even at that price, if you were to get forty diapers (which is a reasonable number of cloth diapers to have on hand so you're not doing laundry every day) you'd spend about the same amount of money or less than you'd spend on disposables for the first year. Still, twenty dollars for one diaper seemed extreme to me.

While I was trying to decide if I could swallow the price tag, I started to familiarize myself with the cloth–diapering options available these days. There are pocket diapers with inserts, fitted diapers, all–in–one diapers, one–size–fits–all diapers, soakers, pre–folds, diaper covers... and the list goes on. I quickly realized that if I was going to spend twenty dollars for one diaper, it had better be as convenient and as long–lasting as possible.

What I was looking for was a cloth diaper that I didn't have to stuff or fold or prepare in any way other than washing it before putting it on my baby. When you boil it down, I was looking for the cloth–diaper equivalent of a disposable. In addition to being incredibly easy to use, I wanted my diapers to be relevant for as long as possible. Having researched the diaper options out there, I realized I was looking for an "all–in–one, one–size–fits–all" cloth diaper.

Except that an all–in–one, one–size–fits–all cloth diaper didn't seem to exist. (There is at least one option out there now, but it still requires special folding as I understand it. When I started this whole quest, there were no commercially available cloth diapers that met my criteria.)

It didn't take long for me to start wondering if I could make cloth diapers myself.

That was the beginning of the saga that led to this book. After a solid year of researching fabrics, experimenting with various designs and materials, and – most importantly – using cloth diapers on my baby, I have come up with the diaper I was looking for in the beginning.

To be clear: this is not a book about making a variety of different kinds of cloth diapers. This is a book focusing on making an all–in–one, one–size–fits–most diaper. I say "most" because a newborn's legs are generally too skinny for these diapers. I started using these diapers on my son when he was two months old, and I anticipate being able to use them for another year or more. At seven months, he's still got ample room to grow into them.

Before I jump in, there is one other thing I'd like to share with you. I wasn't sure at first if I wanted to make the commitment to cloth diaper. If I'm being totally honest, while the environmental impact was something I did think about, I was equally concerned about the amount of money we'd be spending on disposable diapers. Things are lean all around, and if I could save us close to a thousand dollars a year, wouldn't that be worth spending the time to learn how to make and care for cloth diapers?

I'm so glad I did. I can now sincerely and whole–heartedly say that I love cloth diapering. I think some part of that comes from having made these diapers myself.

If you are looking for the same solution I was, I hope this guide saves you the time and headaches I spent getting to this point. Good luck to you, and happy cloth diapering!

Jennifer Berry
October 2011

Jennifer C. Berry

CHAPTER 1:
THE PATTERN

The first challenge with any sewing project is – of course – the pattern.

I looked for a pattern that fit my criteria (an all–in–one, one–size–fits–all cloth diaper), but couldn't find the right pattern "out of the box," so I decided to make a pattern of my own.

In this chapter, I'll take you step–by–step through the process I used to draft the pattern in this book.

What You'll Need:

- large sheet of paper (newsprint, etc.)
- ruler
- pencil
- square (optional)
- tape (optional)
- poster board (optional)

If you're not comfortable with the idea of drafting your own pattern, there are several diaper patterns available online. Some are free and some are available for a few dollars. You can find a pattern whose shape you like and use it with the instructions in this book to create an all-in-one, one-size-fits-most diaper. (See the "Resources" section at the end of this book for some ideas of where to look for diaper patterns.)

STEP 1:

Start by folding a large piece of paper (at least 22 inches x 20 inches) in half length–wise. You'll be creating one half of the pattern against the folded side. This way, when you cut the pattern out, it will be symmetrical. I suggest drawing a 1–inch grid on your paper to make drafting the rest of the pattern easier.

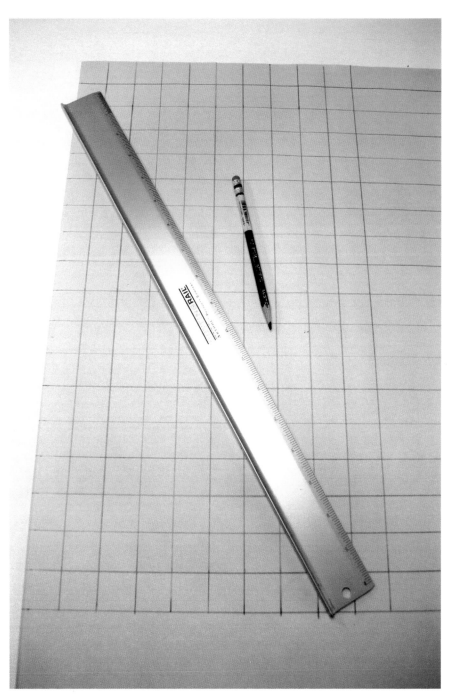

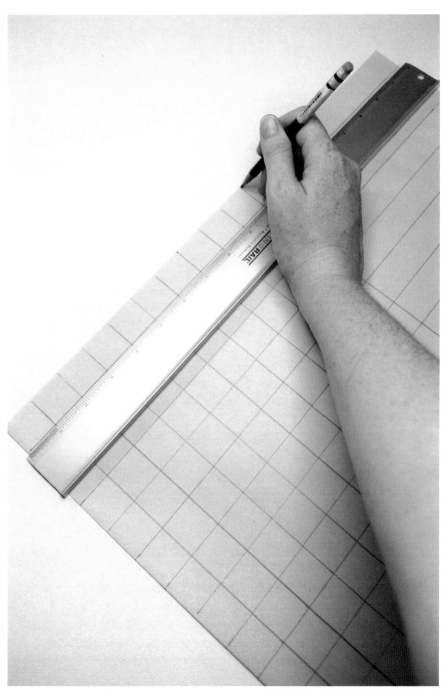

STEP 2:

The back of the diaper pattern should be 20 inches wide. Part of this width will be gathered up when you add the elastic. Measure 10 inches in from the folded edge and make a mark. This edge will be the "back" edge.

STEP 3:

The diaper pattern should be 18 inches long from back to tummy. Measure 18 inches down and make a mark on the folded edge. This will be the "tummy" edge of the pattern.

STEP 4:

The diaper pattern should be 8½ inches across the tummy. Use a ruler to make a mark 4¼ inches in from the fold on the "tummy" edge.

STEP 5:

As you can see in the following photo, you need to create a taper from the tummy down to the fabric that will go between the legs. The absorbent pad you'll be making will be 5 inches wide, so you need to make sure there will be room for the pad to fit.

Taper from 8½ inches at the tummy down to 6½ inches between the legs (this will include the seam allowance). Start the taper 2 inches from the "tummy" edge and finish it 5 inches from the "tummy" edge.

At 2 inches from the "tummy" edge, make a mark at 4¼ inches from the folded edge.

At 5 inches from the "tummy" edge, make a mark at 3¼ inches from the folded edge.

You can divide the inch between your 3¼ inch mark and your 4¼ inch mark into thirds to help create a guide for the taper.

Freehand a line through your marks, trying to create a gentle curve from one to the next. Don't worry if you have to try this several times to get it right – this is all about trial and error.

STEP 6:

As you can see in the following photo, you also need to create a taper from the leg section into the back section.

At 9 inches from the "back" edge, make a mark at 3¼ inches from the folded edge.

At 6½ inches from the "back" edge, make a mark at 4¼ inches from the folded edge.

At 3 inches from the "back" edge, make a mark at 7 inches from the folded edge.

Freehand a nice curve up through these marks. Again, don't worry if you don't get it perfect the first time. Keep at it until you're happy with the result.

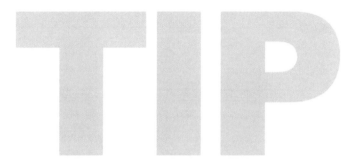

To get a smoother curve, try planting your wrist against the table and pivoting your hand with the pencil in it.

STEP 7:

You'll want the flaps of the diaper to have nice curved edges. You've already marked 10 inches from the folded edge at the top of the pattern. Using that as the outside guide, freehand the curved edge like you see in the following photo.

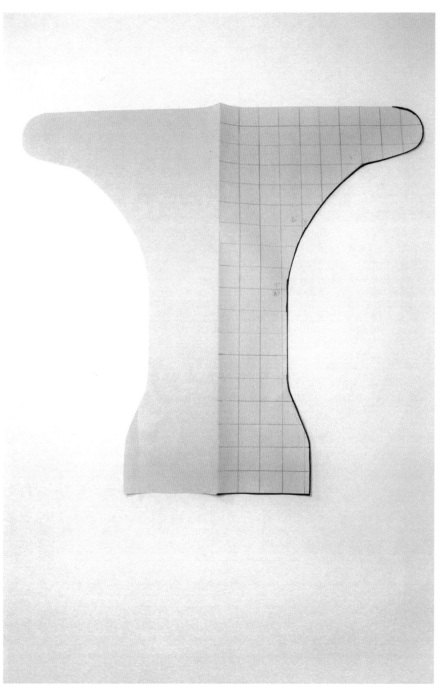

STEP 8:

Take a look at your finished pattern. Now is the time to make any tweaks. (Keep in mind that the back and legs will be gathered up with elastic, so if it looks big to you, don't panic.)

Done? Great! Keeping the paper folded, carefully cut along your pattern edge. Once you are done cutting, you can open the fold and look at your completed diaper pattern.

STEP 9:

This step is optional, but I've found that it makes life much simpler down the road. Take your paper pattern and trace it onto a piece of poster board or other stiff paper. Cut the poster board pattern out. You'll be tracing your pattern over and over, and using this stiff poster board instead of flimsy paper will make the job faster and easier.

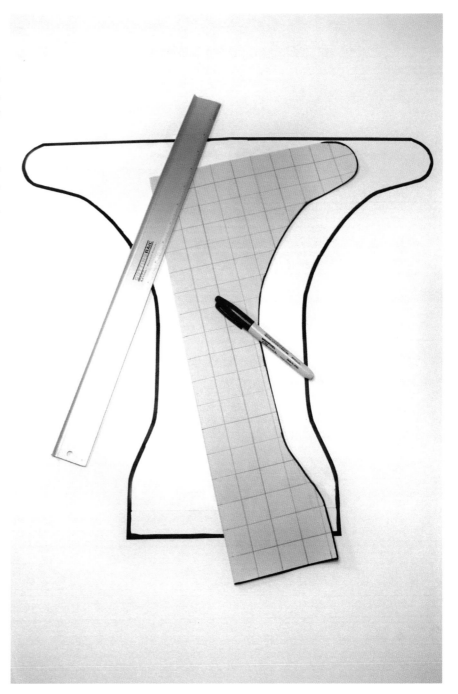

To make storing your pattern easier, try taping two pieces of poster board together and centering your pattern along the seam. This way, when you are ready to put the pattern away, it will fold easily at the taped edge and you won't risk damaging it.

STEP 10:

Now you need to mark where the back elastic will go. Mark 5 inches in from either side with a dot. That will give you 5 inches of flaps on either side with the space in between gathered up by elastic.

(You're going to use 5 inches of elastic for this – so the total length of the back of the finished diaper will be closer to 15 inches.)

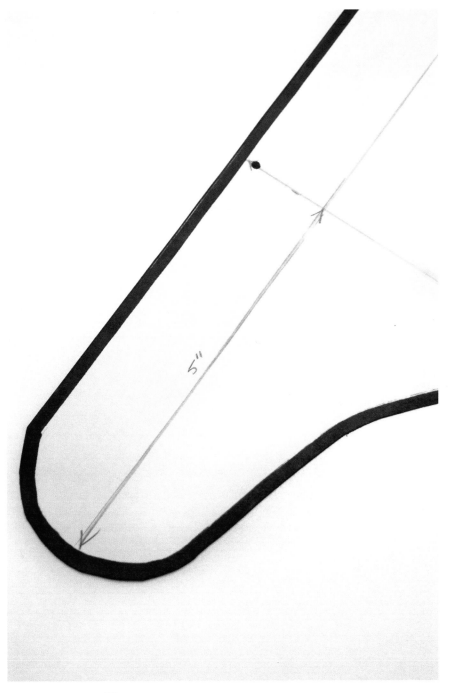

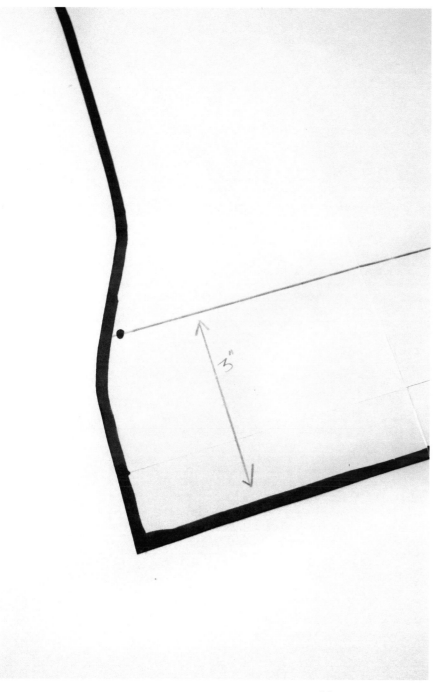

STEP 11:

Likewise, you'll need to mark where the leg elastic will go.

Make a mark on both sides of the diaper at 3 inches from the "tummy" edge.

Make another mark on both sides of the diaper at 4 inches from the "back" edge.

Congratulations! The pattern is done.

Now let's talk about what materials you'll need to get started making your cloth diapers.

CHAPTER 2:
THE MATERIALS

I spent months scouring my local fabric stores (including the expansive fabric district in downtown Los Angeles) for the right materials to make cloth diapers.

Please let me save you a gigantic headache; your best bet is to purchase your fabrics online.

Feel free to go crazy bargain shopping for the notions (thread, elastic, and hook and loop) in your local store.

But the fabrics are another story – you cannot substitute some of these fabrics for "similar" options.

Planning ahead can save you money. If you know you want to make 45 diapers, figure out all your fabric requirements and place your order for everything in one go. You could save a good amount in postage this way.

FABRIC

The right fabrics are crucial to making cloth diapers. If you want to know why the store–bought diapers are so expensive, it's because the right materials don't come cheap.

There are three layers to cloth diapers:

- An external, **waterproof layer**.

- A **lining** that wicks moisture away from the baby's skin.

- An **absorbent layer** to hold moisture.

WATERPROOF LAYER
My Recommendation:
PUL

Almost all the commercial diaper makers use the same fabric for the external layer. It's called PUL (which stands for polyurethane laminated fabric). It's a comfy, stretchy, waterproof material that was originally developed for use in hospitals. This is a fantastic fabric for cloth diapering. In addition to being comfy, stretchy, and waterproof, it's also durable enough to handle being washed repeatedly in hot water. (And as an added bonus, it comes in a variety of colors and patterns!)

The polyurethane laminate is what makes this material waterproof. It is applied to the fabric in a variety of thicknesses, but you'll want to buy the 1 mil variety for cloth diapers. (Some people use the 2 mil variety, but I find that can get bulky.)

Other Waterproof Layer Options:

• Heavyweight Fleece (like Wind Pro®) – (Wind Pro® is a trademark of Polartec®.) This fabric is made of polyester and has waterproof qualities. (Be careful and do your research before you buy – all fleeces are not created equal!)

• ProCare™ – (ProCare™ is a trademark of Wazoodle Fabrics.) According to their website, ProCare™ is a durable waterproof barrier fabric that's used in a wide range of incontinence products, bag linings, and for snack bags.

• ULTREX® – (ULTREX® is a registered trademark of Burlington Industries, Inc.) This is a densely woven, breathable fabric with a micro–porous polyurethane coating and a water repellent finish. It is used primary for outerwear (think rain– or cycling–wear).

• Wool – This fabric is naturally breathable, waterproof, and antibacterial – though it does require special washing.

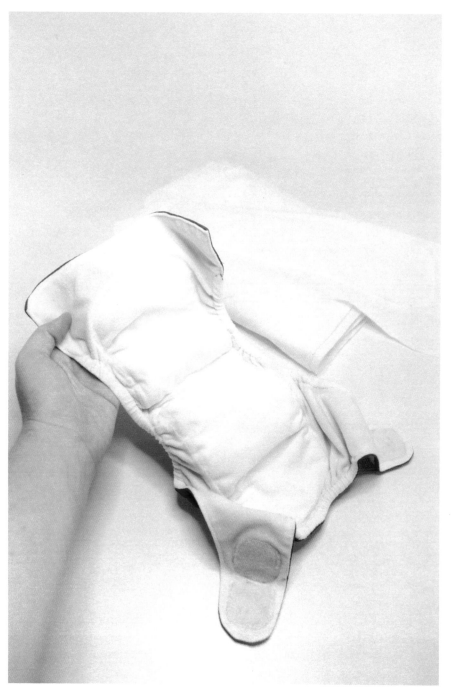

LINING
My Recommendation:
Alova Suede

There are a variety of options available for the inner "wicking" layer ("wicking" means to absorb or draw off liquid). I personally prefer alova suede for many reasons. It's soft on the side touching the baby, it's great at wicking moisture away from the baby's skin, and it doesn't shrink in the dryer. It also resists staining and doesn't pill, which means it stays looking new a lot longer than many other fabrics.

Other Lining Options:

• Lightweight Fleece (like microfleece) – This fabric is made of polyester. It wicks moisture away from the skin to keep the baby dry, and it resists staining.

• Velour – This fabric can be made from cotton or bamboo (and it might have a polyester backing). It tends to be very soft (think velvet).

ABSORBENT LAYER
My Recommendation:
Zorb® (Zorb® is a trademark of Wazoodle Fabrics.)

Fabric options for the absorbent layer range from bamboo to hemp to terry knits. For eco–conscious folks, both bamboo and hemp offer environmentally friendly options that are naturally antibacterial. For the first round of diapers I made, I used hemp. It works, but as my baby grew (and started "outputting" more liquid) I found I needed quite a lot of hemp to keep the diapers from leaking during long naps.

So I was thrilled to hear about a new material whipped up by the design team at Wazoodle (an online source for eco–friendly knitted fabrics and cloth diaper making supplies). It's called Zorb® and – according to the manufacturer – "absorbs 10 times its weight in less than half a second — that's 20 times faster than cotton, bamboo or hemp. Zorb® has incredible holding power too, a single layer holds up to 3 times the moisture of the best absorbing knits." What this translates to is fewer leaks and a more comfortable baby. I've experimented with other fabrics, but Zorb® is hands–down my favorite.

Other Absorbent Layer Options:

- Bamboo – This fabric is pretty absorbent, naturally antibacterial, and environmentally friendly.

- Birdseye – This fabric is made of cotton. Birdseye has an open weave (think gauze) that makes the fabric breathable and pretty absorbent (you might recognize this as the material used in old–school prefold diapers).

- Burley Knit Terry Diaper Fabric (aka BKT) – This fabric is very absorbent and thicker than regular terry. It can get a bit bulky.

- Flannel – This fabric is usually made of cotton or wool. It's pretty absorbent, inexpensive, and easy to find at most local fabric stores.

- Hemp – This fabric is usually a blend of hemp and cotton. It is naturally antimicrobial, and it's stronger and more absorbent than the same weight of cotton fabric.

- Microfiber – This fabric is a blend of polyester and polyamide. It is very absorbent, light, and not bulky. (I've been warned not to use this fabric as a liner – it can dry out your baby's skin).

- Sherpa – This fabric is a pretty absorbent cotton knit terry that's been brushed to create a soft surface on the loop side. (This is also a good fabric for baby wipes, if you're interested in making your own.)

That covers the hard part: fabric selection. Let's take a look at the other odds and ends you'll need to get started making your own cloth diapers.

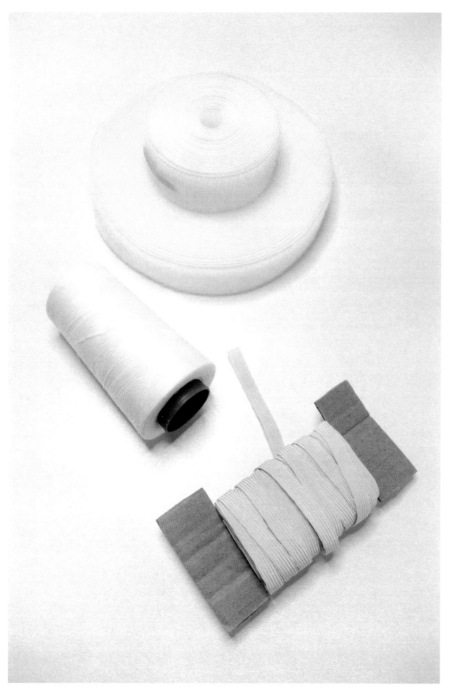

NOTIONS

What you'll need:

- hook & loop
- elastic
- thread

HOOK & LOOP

Most people think of Velcro® when they think of hook and loop. (Velcro® is a trademark of Velcro Industries B.V.) Velcro® is a brand name of hook-and-loop fasteners, but there are a variety of other types of hook and loop out there. The hook and loop is what's going to keep the diaper fastened. You want enough hook and loop contact to make a good connection, but not so much that you're wasting materials.

You can find a variety of colors and sizes of hook and loop out there. I like 1½ inch wide white hook and loop for cloth diapers. You're welcome to experiment with different colors, of course!

You'll need about 3 inches of hook and 16 inches of loop for each diaper.

ELASTIC

There are many different kinds of elastic available, but we're looking for something nice and durable. Braided elastic is a strong choice for cloth diapers. It's tougher than knitted elastic, while still being relatively thin. This elastic is going around tiny legs, so you don't want it to be too wide or uncomfortable. ⅜ inch is a good size for cloth diapers.

You'll need about 18 inches of elastic for each diaper.

THREAD

The quality of thread you use is important. If your thread isn't up to par, your diapers will suffer. This is not a place to save a few cents. I recommend 100% polyester thread to hold up over the long term.

For a professional, finished look, you'll want thread to match each color of diaper you make. (I use white alova suede for the lining of all my diapers, but for the outer waterproof layer I've experimented with a good variety of colors of PUL.)

It's worth noting that cones of thread are quite a bit less expensive than spools. You can get 5000 yards on a cone for around $5.00, while a spool can cost you $2.50 or more for just 250 yards.

To use a cone with a standard sewing machine, you'll need a thread cone holder. Place the cone of thread on the holder, feed the thread through the holder's hook, through your machine's top thread guide, and **then** thread the machine as you would with a regular spool.

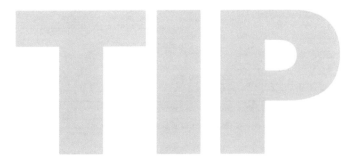

If you use white thread for the majority of the diaper assembly, you'll only need to buy one spool of colored thread for the last step (for up to 20 diapers).

SHOPPING LIST

With this pattern, you should be able to get 15 diapers out of 2 yards of PUL. If you're ready to take the cloth diapering plunge, I'd recommend making 45 diapers. As I've mentioned before, that should give you enough diapers on hand so that you don't find yourself doing laundry every day. (With 45 diapers, I do a load of diapers every 3 or 4 days.)

Once again, you'll save a lot of money on shipping if you buy all of your materials in one big order.

Here's what you'll need for each set of 15 diapers:

- 2 yards of 60–inch wide PUL

- 2 yards of 60–inch wide alova suede (or your lining fabric of choice)

- 2½ yards of 45–inch wide Zorb® (or your absorbent layer of choice)

- 2 yards 1½–inch wide hook

- 7 yards 1½–inch wide loop

- 8 yards ⅜–inch braided elastic

- 1 cone of white thread

- 1 spool (or cone) of thread to match the color of the PUL fabric you've chosen

Make sure you pay attention to the width of the fabrics you buy. Many fabrics come in different widths, from 30–inch to 60–inch. If you by 60–inch wide PUL and 45–inch wide lining, you'll need more yards of lining to complete 15 diapers. (Currently the greatest width of Zorb® you can buy online is 45–inch.)

There are a lot of great online retailers who specialize in diaper–making fabrics and notions. Check the "Resources" section at the end of this book for some options. (I've personally bought from W.A.H.M. Sewing Supply Store (www.wahmsupply.com) many times and have always been 100% satisfied with my order.)

Happy fabric hunting! If you're anything like me, once you put the order in, you'll be on pins and needles until it arrives. I hate waiting, but I love getting that package in the mail.

Next up: the work begins.

Jennifer C. Berry

CHAPTER 3:
SEWING

I know, I know. You want to jump right in and get to sewing. Believe me, I understand! However, if you do some prep work first, the whole process will go more smoothly (and more quickly).

PREP WORK

What you'll need:

- fabric pen or ballpoint pen (to copy the pattern to your fabric)
- ruler
- fabric shears
- quarter
- rotary cutter (optional)
- cutting mat (optional)
- a few sheets of paper (optional)

First, prewash your PUL and alova suede in hot water. You do not need to use soap in this wash. Do not iron your fabrics (especially the alova suede – it might melt).

You're now beginning the process of mass–producing cloth diapers. Like an assembly line, it will be more efficient to focus on one task at a time. So steel yourself – you're in for a lot of cutting.

I made my first 30 or so diapers with a pair of decent–but–not–great shears. Then I received a pair of really good dressmaking shears for my birthday. The difference was instant and remarkable. If you can afford it, invest in a pair of good dressmaking shears. Your hands will thank you.

CUTTING THE WATERPROOF & LINING LAYERS

You've invested a good bit of money in this fabric, so I know you want to get as much out of it as possible. Start by laying your fabric wrong–side–up on a table. (For PUL, this will be the shiny side. For alova suede, it will be the non–fuzzy side.)

Lay your pattern with the "back" edge on the cut edge of your fabric. If you bought 60–inch wide fabric, you should be able to trace 3 diapers along the bottom of the fabric. It's okay for the edges to touch – we've included the seam allowance in the pattern.

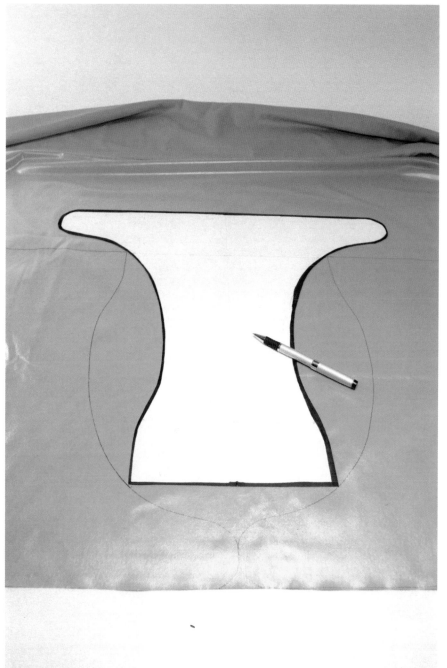

Once you've got the first row of diapers traced onto the fabric, turn your pattern so the "tummy" edge faces the cut edge of your fabric. Line it up so that the "tummy" edge fits between two of the diaper patterns you just traced. Slide the pattern as low as you can without overlapping the lines you traced on the first row. You should be able to fit two diapers on this second row.

You will repeat this pattern up the length of the fabric. You should be able to get 3 sets of 5 diapers (or – yes, basic math time – 15 diapers) out of 2 yards of 60–inch fabric. Do this for both the PUL fabric and the lining fabric.

Once you've traced all the diapers onto the fabric, carefully cut them out.

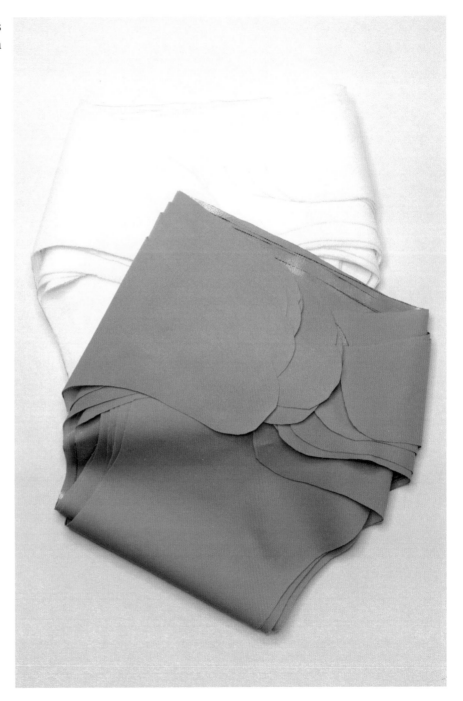

MARKING THE LINING LAYER

When you've finished cutting the patterns out, take a moment to copy the elastic anchor points onto the lining fabric. As with the pattern, you'll make these marks on the wrong side of the fabric. (NOTE: you do not need to copy the elastic anchor points to the PUL fabric).

CUTTING THE ABSORBENT PADS

There's one good thing about the 45–inch width of the Zorb® fabric: you're making absorbent pads that are 5x15 inches and three layers thick. You can cut 5–inch strips that are 45 inches long. Then, instead of cutting each layer to 5x15 inches, you can simply fold the 5x45–inch strips in thirds to sew. (We'll cover sewing the pads in a moment).

Using a rotary cutter and a metal ruler can make this process much faster. Make sure you put a cutting mat or a piece of cardboard under your fabric to protect the surface of your table from the rotary blade. And – of course – take care not to cut yourself!

CUTTING THE HOOK & LOOP

For each diaper you'll need:

- 2 – 1½–inch squares of hook
- 2 – 1½–inch squares of loop
- 2 – 3–inch lengths of loop
- 1 – 7–inch length of loop

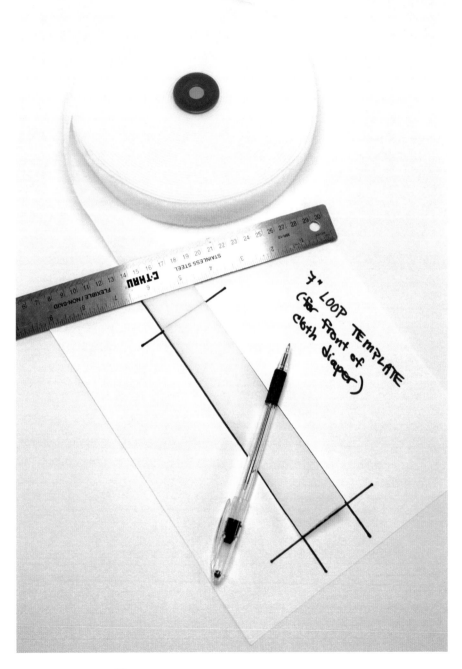

Drawing a few templates on a sheet of paper can make this step go more quickly. Draw two sets of perpendicular lines. Make one 1½ inch wide (the width of the hook and loop). Make the other the width of the pieces you need to cut (3 inches, 7 inches, etc.). Then simply line your hook or loop up, line the ruler up, and draw a line along the back of the hook or loop at the correct length.

Once you've marked up the hook and loop, cut the individual pieces out. Notice that the corners are a little sharp. Since you're putting these on little ones, you'll want to blunt those edges by cutting curves around the corners of each piece.

One quick and easy way to get nice, matching corners is to line a quarter up in each corner to act as a guide. Trace the edge of the quarter onto the back of the hook or loop to get a consistent curve, and then cut along the guides.

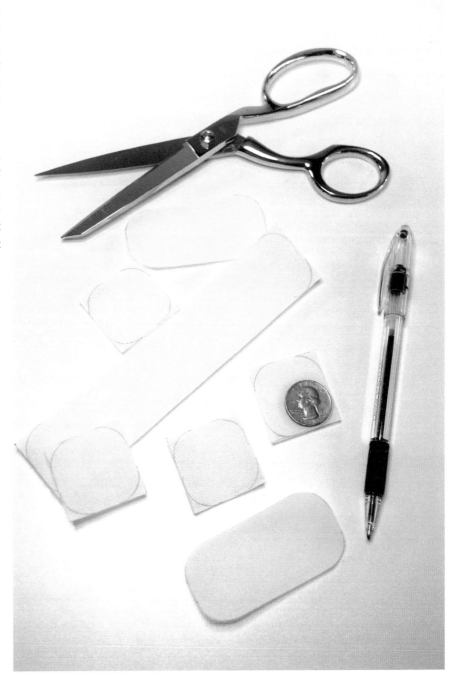

I like to store the bits in little bags or bins to keep them organized. Then when I'm sewing, I don't have to interrupt my flow to stop and cut anything out – I have it all ready to go. Additionally, I like to pair the 1½–inch hook and loop pieces together. It's a quick and easy way to make sure you have the right number of pieces, and it keeps the hook from getting lost or stuck to other pieces of loop.

MARKING THE ELASTIC

Don't cut the elastic before sewing it.

You'll need something to hold onto as you're running the elastic through the machine. However, you can prepare the elastic by marking the segments you'll need for each diaper.

Measure segments like this: 5 inches (for the back), 6½ inches (for one leg), and 6½ inches (for the other leg). This is the order in which you'll sew the elastic onto the diaper. Repeat this pattern along the length of the elastic until you have marked 15 complete sets.

(Again, do not cut the elastic yet!)

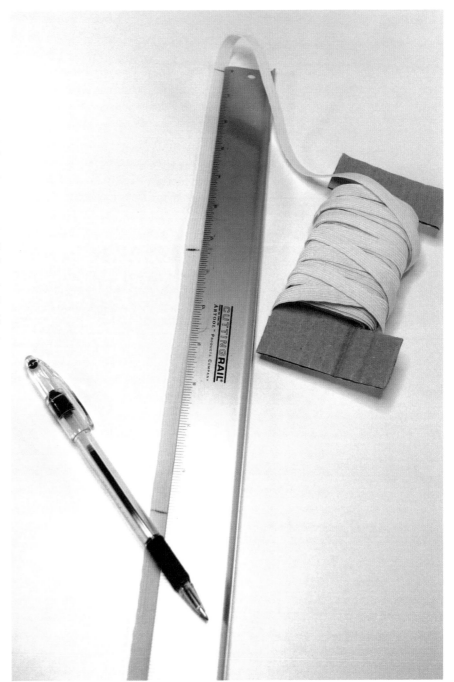

SEWING

Now you're ready to start sewing your diapers. Whether you craft one diaper at a time or do the assembly–line trick of performing each step on all diapers before you move onto the next step is up to you. (I usually do one set of 15 diapers (by color) at a time, assembly–line–style.)

What you'll need:

- sewing machine
- stick pins
- fabric shears or snips
- seam ripper (optional but useful)
- serger (optional)

If I can offer a quick word of advice: pin. Pin (almost) everything. Many of the stitches we'll be working with are small and tightly spaced – in other words, a real pain to pick out if you make a mistake. Pinning can help minimize mistakes.

Before you start, thread white thread into the machine (spool and bobbin). You'll be able to do most of the diaper assembly with white thread, so you won't have to keep changing out thread colors.

STEP 1:

Take your 5x45–inch strips of Zorb® (or absorbent material of choice) and fold them into thirds in an "S" pattern. Pin the fabric together. Freehand curves on the edges and cut them out. These don't have to be perfect – once you sew them into the diaper no one will ever see them.

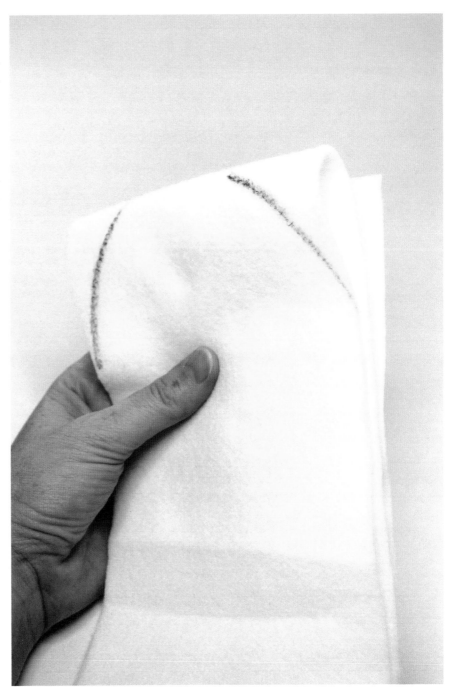

STEP 2:

Using a wide zigzag stitch, go around the edge of the fabric a few times to hold everything together.

If you have a serger, this is a perfect time to break it out. I find I don't need to pin the three layers with the serger, but I do need to make sure to keep the pad flat so it doesn't curl up anywhere. You don't need to cut the corners if you have a serger, you can let the blade cut them for you.

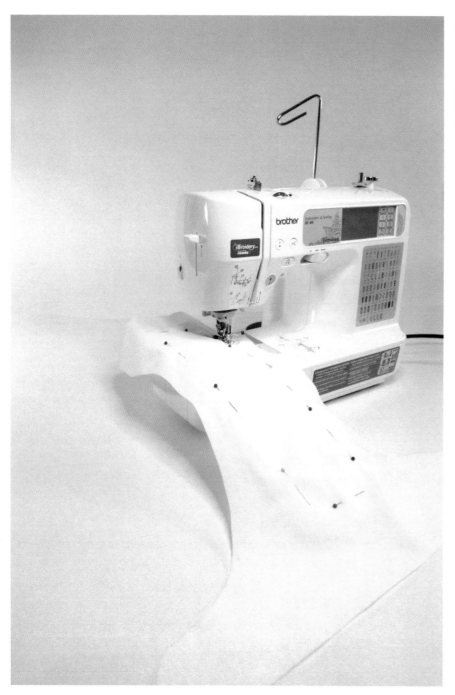

STEP 3:

Pin the absorbent pad to the wrong side of the lining fabric. Place it 2 inches down from the "tummy" edge. Sew the pad to the lining using a wide zigzag stitch.

Through trial and error I've discovered that this step will be much easier to sew if you put the absorbent pad down and then pin the lining (right side up) on top of it. This will help keep the pad from slipping in the machine.

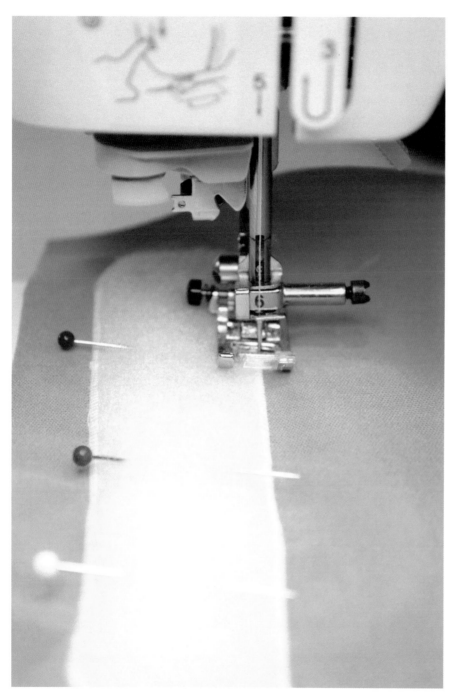

STEP 4:

Pin the 7–inch piece of loop to the right side of the PUL fabric. It should be centered on the front of the diaper, ¾ of an inch down from the "tummy" edge. Set your sewing machine to a small, tight zigzag pattern, and sew around the loop. PUL can be tricky to work with, but the pins should help keep the loop from shifting around too much on the fabric. Go slowly until you get the feel for it.

STEP 5:

Pin the PUL and the alova suede together, right sides facing in. Set your machine to a straight stitch. Use the guide marks on your machine to sew a ⅜–inch seam. (I line my fabric up to the edge of my presser foot, which gives me the right distance.) Start at the "tummy" edge. Anchor your stitch (sew back and forth a few times), then (leaving a ⅜–inch seam allowance) sew down one leg, around the back, and up the other leg.

Leave the "tummy" edge open, you'll be turning the diaper right–side out through this opening in a moment.

Go slowly around the rounded edges of the flaps – they will look much nicer if you keep an even seam around the curve. When you reach the end of the diaper, anchor your stitch at this end as well.

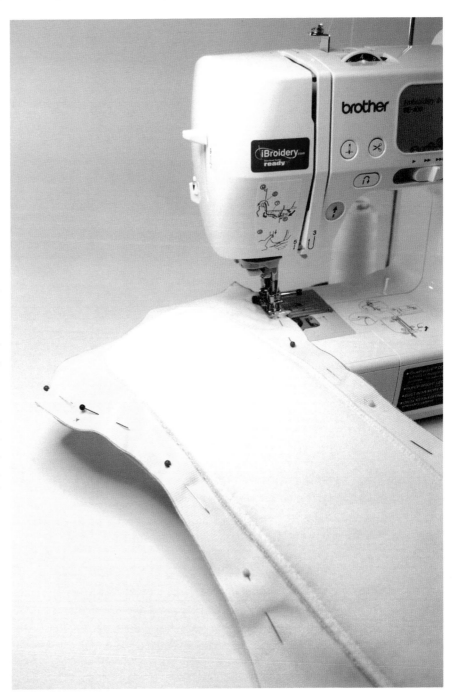

You can avoid a lot of frustration if you pin these fabrics together with the alova suede on top. The PUL will slip and slide all over the place if it's on top.

STEP 6:

Now you're going to sew the elastic into the diaper. Start with the back elastic. This is the 5–inch segment we measured earlier. Set your sewing machine to a wide zigzag stitch. Anchor the edge of the elastic at the first anchor point. You want to rest the elastic up against the "back" edge – you'll be sewing the elastic onto the seam allowance. Stretch the elastic until the mark reaches the second anchor point. While holding the elastic stretched, carefully sew the elastic onto the diaper. Anchor the elastic at the second anchor point as well. Then clip the elastic.

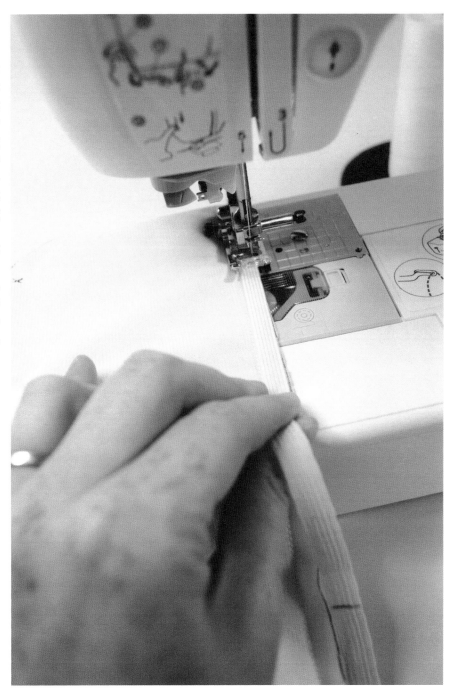

STEP 7:

Repeat this process with the elastic on both legs. It might be a bit harder to maintain a consistent stretch on the legs since the material is curved. Do the best you can. Remember to anchor the elastic at both the beginning and ending anchor points. When you're done, your diaper will be bunched up at the legs and back.

STEP 8:

You're almost ready to turn the diaper right side out – but before you do, take a moment to cut off any loose threads and clip the curves of the flaps so they'll lay flatter when you turn them. I generally clip the curves in three places.

STEP 9:

Turn the diaper right side out, making sure to push the curves all the way out. It's starting to look like a diaper, but there's still a little ways to go.

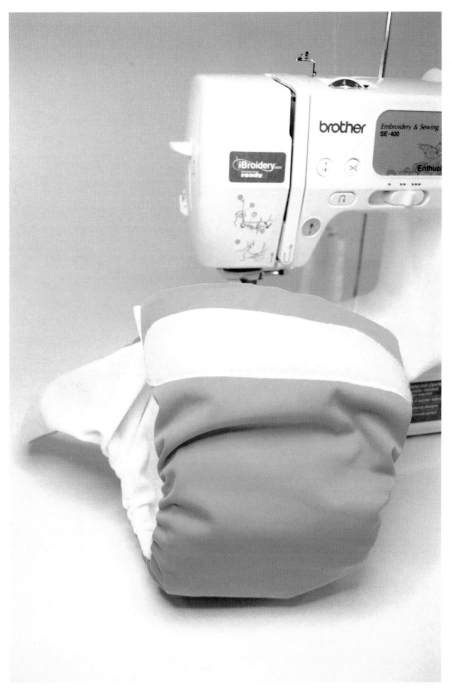

STEP 10:

Sew one of the 1½–inch hook squares onto the lining side of the diaper, centering it so that you get a relatively even spacing around it (it should be around ¼ of an inch from the "back" edge of the diaper). Set your sewing machine to a small, tight zigzag stitch (the same stitch you used to sew the loop to the front of the diaper in step three). Sew the hook square in place. Repeat this on the other flap.

Note: steps 10 through 12 are the only times I recommend sewing without pinning, because the pieces are so small that it's easier to hold them in place.

STEP 11:

Leave a small space (around ¼ of an inch) and sew the matching 1 ½–inch loop square next to the hook square the same way, aligning it ¼ inch from the "back" edge of the diaper as well. Repeat this on the other flap.

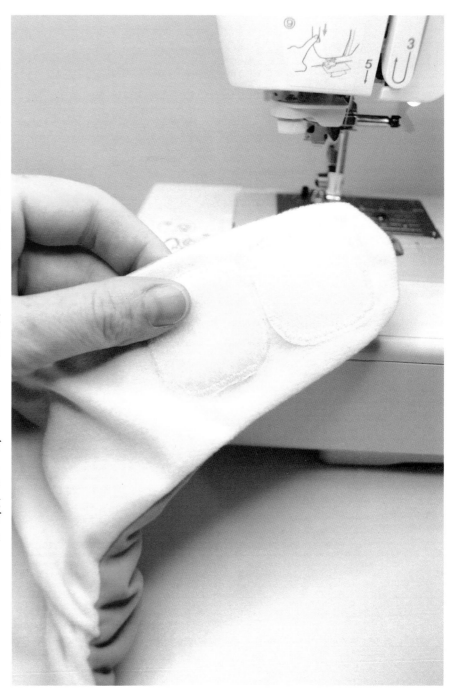

I recommend sewing slightly inside the hook and loop pieces (instead of right at the edge) in these two steps. The reason for this is that you'll be sewing the 3–inch loop piece on the other side of this flap in a little while, and you want it to cover the stitches from these pieces to give the diaper a nicer finished look.

STEP 12:

Sew one of the 3–inch loop pieces to the PUL side of the diaper flap. Carefully line it up to cover the stitches from steps 10 and 11. Use the same small, tight, zigzag stitch. Repeat this on the other flap with the other 3–inch loop piece.

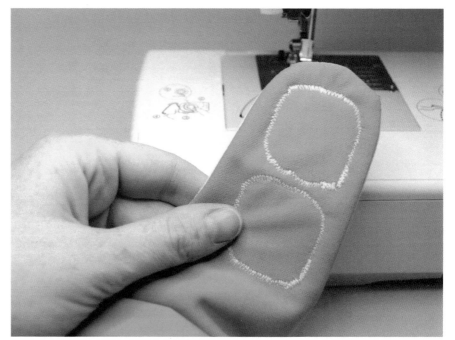

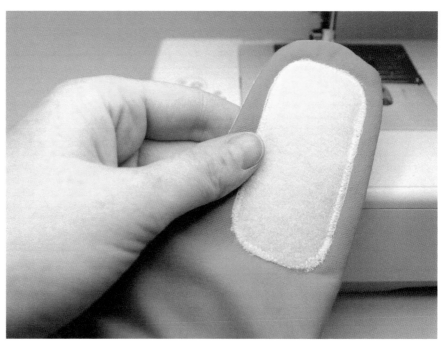

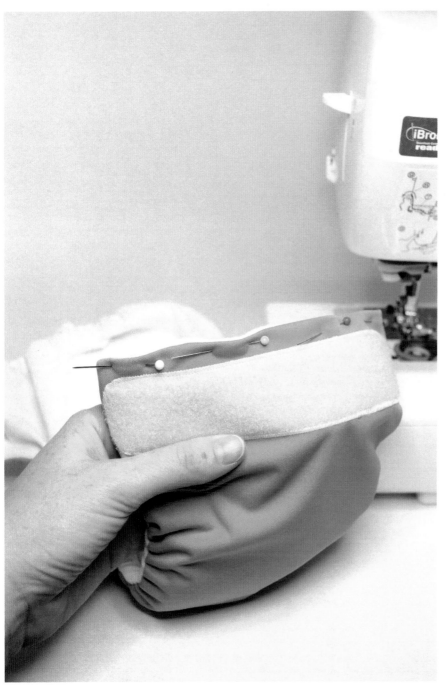

STEP 13:

Fold the fabric in and pin the "tummy" edge closed.

Note: This time, you want to pin with the PUL on top and the lining underneath.

As you're folding and pinning, ease the fabric between your fingers until it lays flat. You might have to fold more lining or PUL to get a nice even edge, but this will ensure the edge lays flat later on (really an aesthetic issue – it won't affect the performance of the diaper!)

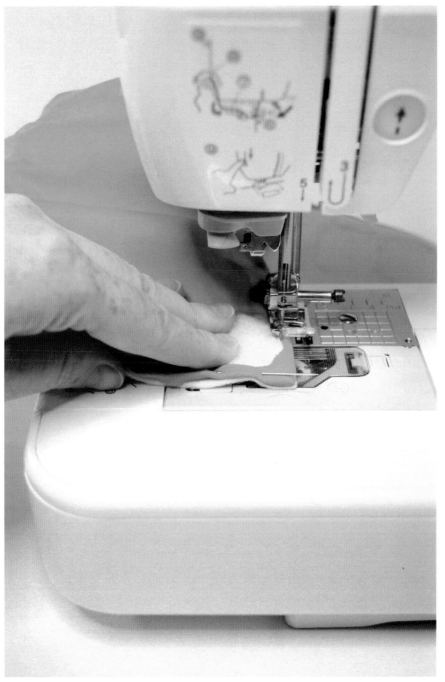

STEP 14:

Change your upper thread to the color that matches your PUL fabric. The bobbin thread can remain white. Set your machine to a straight stitch.

STEP 15:

Now it's time for the finishing step: sewing a seam around the diaper.

Starting just above the elastic anchor point of the right leg, sew toward the "tummy" edge (remembering to anchor at the start of your stitch). You want this seam to be close to the edge.

Stop at the corner, reinforce your stitch, and sew across the tummy, taking care to create a nice, even seam as you sew the "tummy" edge closed. Sew down the other side of the diaper.

When you get to the first piece of leg elastic, increase the seam distance. You want to stretch the elastic taut. The idea is to sew close to the elastic without catching any of the elastic in your seam. This will give you a nice finished look at the leg. I like to anchor my seam before and after each piece of elastic, just to reinforce the diaper.

Continue around the diaper, with a narrow seam that expands when you get to the next piece of elastic. When you make it all the way back to your starting point, anchor your stitch and clip your thread.

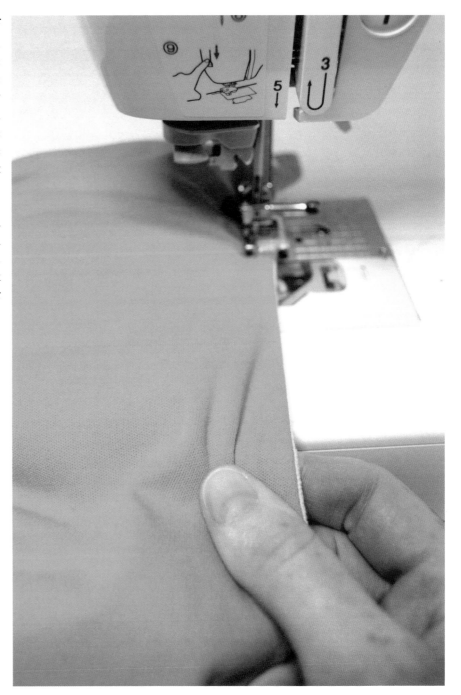

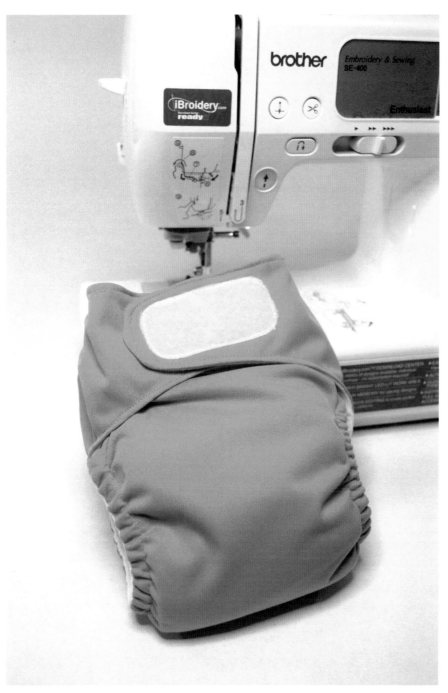

STEP 16:

Wash your diapers in hot water once before you use them. I made the mistake of skipping this step once. Learn from me and save yourself an extra baby change. I know I've already waxed poetic about how amazing PUL is, but I left one thing out: it is also self–healing. In constructing these diapers, you just put hundreds of tiny holes in your waterproof fabric. When you wash PUL in hot water, those holes should close up. If you don't wash your diapers before you use them, those holes don't close up… and you'll have a leaky baby bum to prove it.

Take a moment to admire your handy work: your diaper is finished.

CHAPTER 4:
DIAPER USE & CARE

Now that you've taken the time and energy to make these cloth diapers, it's worth taking a moment to talk about how to use and care for them – and before you panic, let me assure you it's a whole lot easier than you probably think!

First, let's talk about how to use these diapers.

USE

By design (if you'll remember, this was one of my primary missions!) these diapers work very similarly to disposable diapers.

That basically means they should always be ready to use straight out of the dryer with no special stuffing, folding, or arranging necessary.

The hook & loop tabs should provide a nice and secure attachment, even after repeated washings. (As of this printing, I've been using my cloth diapers for over 11 months and they are holding up beautifully.)

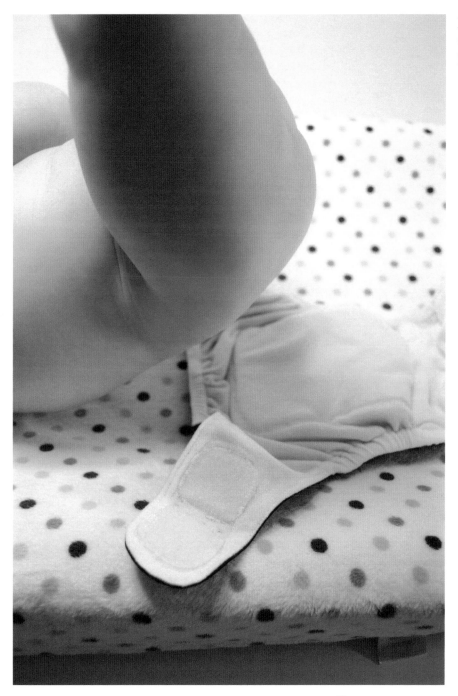

Lift up your baby's feet and place the "back" edge of the diaper under his or her bum.

Lift the tummy portion up between your baby's legs and wrap the flaps around.

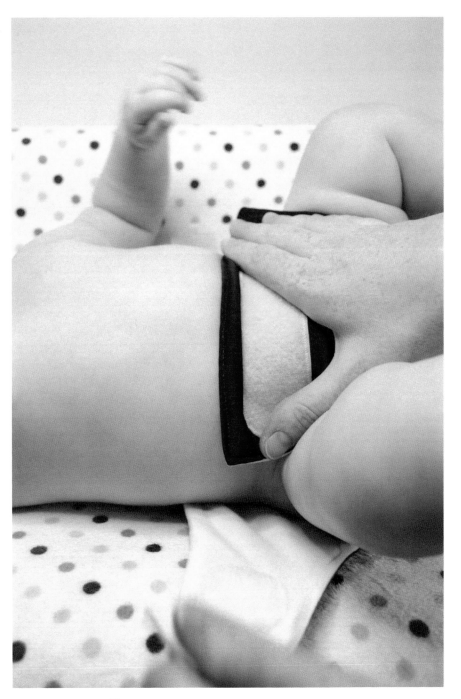

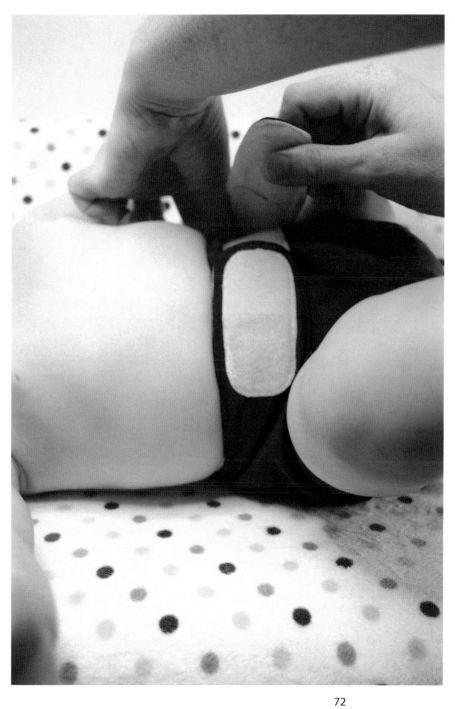

The hook will attach to the loop on the tummy to keep the diaper fastened.

When your baby is small, you can overlap the tabs. The first tab will attach to the tummy loop. The second tab will attach to the loop on the back of the first tab. As your baby grows, simply fasten the tabs further apart.

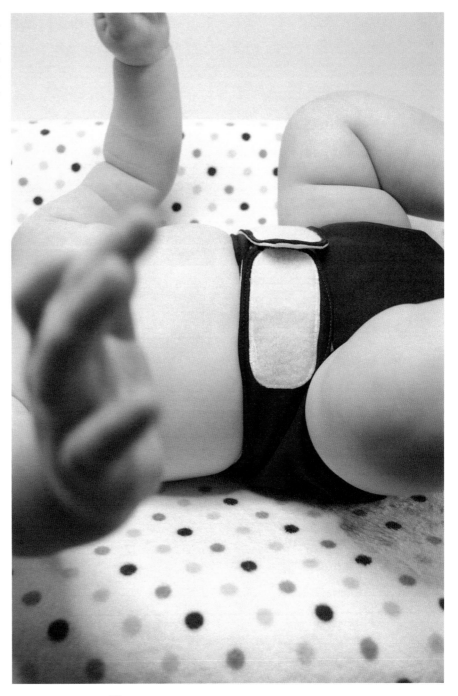

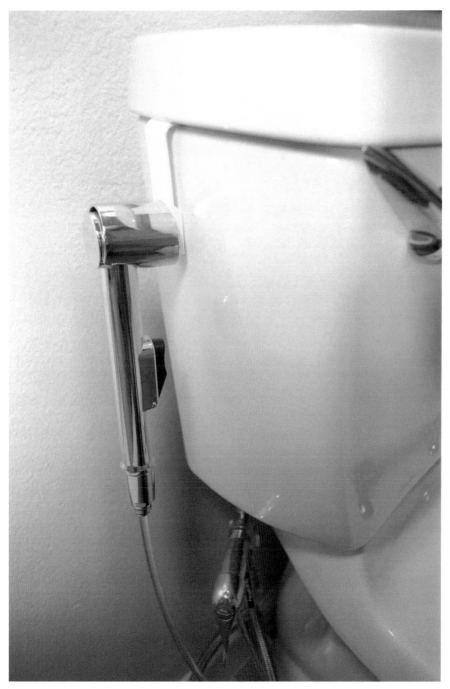

CARE

There are a lot of products out there to help you maintain and clean cloth diapers, but I've found I only need a few things to keep my diapers in great condition:

DIAPER SPRAYER

This is a small, hand–held sprayer that attaches to the back of your toilet. You can use it to spray solids into your toilet and flush them away. This keeps the majority of baby poop out of your washing machine. (Which – I hope we can all agree – is a pretty outstanding goal.) Experiment with the spray pressure – you don't want it so forceful that it sprays all over your bathroom, but you want it strong enough to clean all the solid material off your diapers.

DIAPER PAILS & LINERS

There are a bunch of different systems for cloth diapers. Some people use "wet pails" some use "dry pails." I opted for the easiest system I could find. I use two dry pails.

In the nursery I have a large Dekor diaper pail for wet diapers.

In the bathroom I have a smaller Safety First diaper pail for the dirty diapers after I spray them. This one has a space in it for an air freshener (I use Munchkin Arm and Hammer Nursery Fresheners). I don't know if it's the freshener or the fact that I spray the diapers, but we've never had an odor problem – even when our son started eating solid foods).

I use Kissaluvs Antibacterial Pail Liners for both pails, and I really like them. I just throw the liner into the wash along with the diapers when I do a load.

DIAPER RASH CREAMS

Don't use any diaper rash cream containing mineral oil or zinc oxide with cloth diapers. These creams protect the baby's skin by creating a moisture–proof barrier, but when they rub off on cloth diapers they can cause the diaper lining itself to be moisture–resistant – and we want the diapers to absorb not repel moisture!

Instead of a zinc oxide ointment, I use the Gro Via Magic Stick All Natural Diaper Ointment – but there are a lot of cloth–diaper safe options out there.

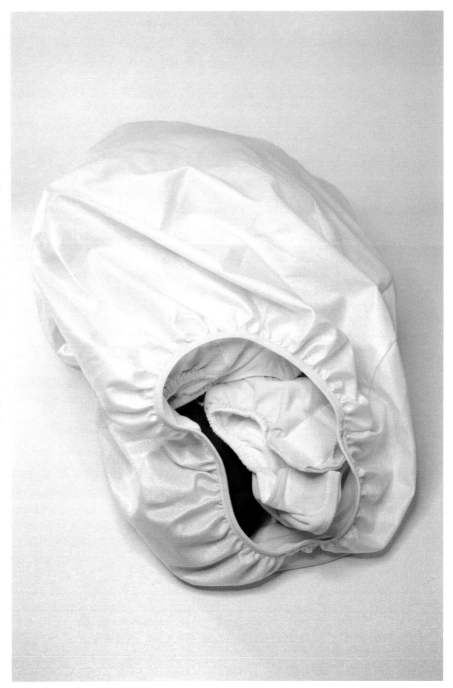

LAUNDERING

Here's what I do to keep my diapers fresh and clean:

First, I fold each diaper flap over so that the hook square touches the loop square. This keeps the hook from catching on other diapers and potentially damaging them.

I dump all my diapers (and the pail liners when necessary) into my washing machine and wash them on the whitest whites setting with two tablespoons of Rockin' Green Hard Rock Laundry Detergent (the "Bare Naked Babies" version is unscented). Alternatively, you can use your regular baby detergent – just use ¼ of the recommended amount. Don't use fabric softeners with your cloth diapers.

If anything starts to smell funky, I simply soak my diapers in the washing machine for 35 minutes with a scoop of Baby OxiClean® and then do a normal wash.

I have a high efficiency washing machine, which makes laundering cloth diapers just a bit trickier (though you do use less soap!). These are incredibly absorbent diapers, so when I soak them in my HE washing machine I have to add more water because the diapers want to soak it all up. I have a little watering can that I fill and pour three or four times into the detergent compartment. If you use a top–loader, you probably won't have this problem.

To dry, you can either put them in the dryer (no dryer sheets!), or hang them up outside. If you do find your diapers seem to be staining, lay them out in the sun for a few hours. The sun should bleach the stain away.

Beyond that, I simply fold them up and they're ready for the next diaper change. Nothing to stuff and no elaborate folding necessary. In my opinion, they are as easy to use as disposables. I figure it takes just a little more time to do laundry than it would to go to the store to buy more diapers. And it saves a lot of money.

Not to mention, if we ever have another baby, we'll have the diapers ready to go.

CHAPTER 5:
ODDS & ENDS

Congratulations! You now have a whole pile of cloth diapers. And – most likely – a whole pile of scraps.

Before you throw those scraps away, here's a few things you might want to consider making:

LUNCH BAGS

For the price of a few zippers and some lining material (simple cotton fabric works great), you can make reusable sandwich bags with your left over PUL.

NURSING PADS

Containing leaks doesn't stop with the baby. Using the lid of a large jar, trace out circles on your PUL, lining, and any left over Zorb®. It's the same idea as the diapers: lining against the skin, absorbent layer to wick moisture, waterproof layer to keep moisture contained.

WET DIAPER BAGS

If you travel with cloth diapers, you'll want a waterproof bag to store wet and dirty diapers. You could simply use PUL to make the bag, or you could use your PUL as a liner and use any fabric you like as the outer layer. You'll need a zipper to keep the bag closed.

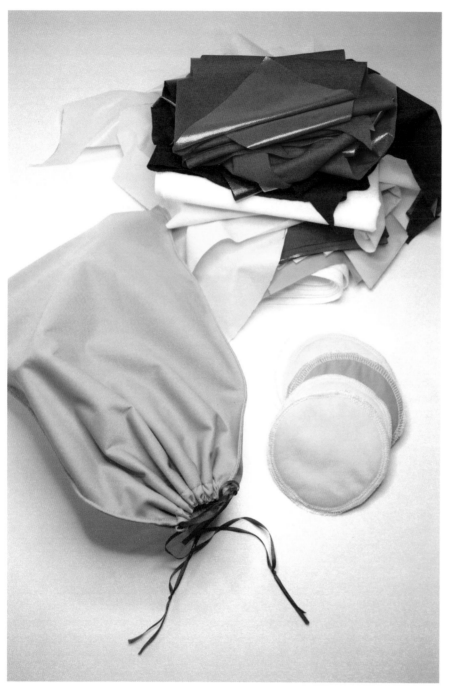

BREAST PUMP PARTS BAGS

If you have to pump during your job, you can make a handy bag for storing your breast pump parts for the trips to and from work. I made one with some drawstrings. It's handy, waterproof to keep any liquids contained, and easy to wash.

SWIMMING SUIT BAG

Make a waterproof bag to toss your wet suits into when you're travelling.

Go ahead, get creative! I'm betting you can come up with even more ideas for those scraps.

And with that, we've come to the end of this little book. I wish you luck with your cloth diapering. I hope it gives you the same level of satisfaction it's given me.

Jennifer C. Berry

RESOURCES

MATERIAL SUPPLIERS:

Celtic Cloths
http://www.celticclothswholesale.com/

Diapercuts
http://www.diapercuts.com/

Very Baby
http://verybaby.com/

W.A.H.M. Sewing Supply Store
http://www.wahmsupply.com/

Wazoodle
http://www.wazoodle.com/
Home of DiaperMaker™ materials specifically designed for use in diapers (including PUL, elastics, linings, Zorb®, Zorb II™, and ProCare™).

DiaperCoop™
http://DiaperCoop.com
A website for cooperative diaper supply buying.

DIAPER PATTERNS:

The Diaper Jungle is a good resource with a super handy list of diaper patterns: http://www.diaperjungle.com/sewing-cloth-diapers.html

Zany Zebra Designs is another great resource with even more diaper patterns listed: http://www.zany-zebra.com/free-cloth-diaper-patterns.shtml

ABOUT THE AUTHOR

Jennifer C. Berry is a copywriter, technical writer, and author. She has worked for a variety of companies including Yahoo! Education, Vantage Media, and Vertafore. She loves to create interesting, useful, and beautiful things - from cloth diapers to Elizabethan costumes. She lives in Los Angeles with her husband, her son, and two wily cats.

Made in the USA
San Bernardino, CA
13 July 2013